The very title of Mrs. Coleman's book (*The Wonderful Land of Affliction*) suggests it might promise too much. Nevertheless, she has accomplished what the title promises—and more. Not only will this book paint a picture of the pilgrimage of those who struggle with chronic illness (and remind you that those who struggle for years in the land of affliction often have an extremely close walk with God), but it may also give those who dwell in the land of ease genuine empathy and compassion for those who walk in the land of affliction. Pick up this book and read it—you will be blessed!

Bryan D. Estelle, Ph.D.
Professor of Old Testament at Westminster Seminary California

How many authors open their book by admitting, "I was blessed with the gift of gab but not for writing"? Her admission is true: Barbara Coleman is neither a Jane Austin nor an Elizabeth Barrett Browning. But what a loss for Jane and Elizabeth! For while their eloquence stirs the heart, Barbara's simplicity pierces the soul. Her pen is an arrow, and if you are willing, it will pierce you for the better.

Steve Estes
Pastor and Co-author of *When God Weeps*

I want to give this powerful little book to everyone I know! At first, *The Wonderful Land of Affliction* may sound contradictory (Who thinks of affliction as wonderful?). Still, as Barbara masterfully walks with us through the experiences of various characters in the Land of Affliction, you will marvel at how God meets and sustains them. Through the stories of their lives, you will discover that you can draw even deeper into the heart of Christ in your own trials, no matter what they are. Read this book and be encouraged that hope and infinite treasure await in the Land of Affliction!

Vaneetha Risner
Author of *Desperate for Hope*

What is it like to suffer silently as part of the body of Christ while the rest of the church seems to move on without you? In *The Wonderful Land of Affliction*, Barbara Coleman offers a little glimpse of this experience (which is far more common than many realize). Through a creative *Pilgrim's-Progress*-like allegory, Barbara draws on her own experience to bring the story of chronic sufferers to life in a captivating tale that enables empathy, compels compassion, and helps all of God's people better understand and care for those among us dealing with all manner of physical, mental, emotional, and spiritual limitations and struggles.

Dr. S. A. Fix, M.Div. Westminster Seminary California; Ph.D.
The Catholic University of America, Pastor, adjunct faculty at Westminster Theological Seminary (PA), Reformed Theological Seminary (DC), and Faith Theological Seminary (MD).

Barbara Coleman's *The Wonderful Land of Affliction* gives a heartfelt, birds-eye view of the joys and sorrows of those afflicted with chronic illness. In a world full of pain and suffering, this thought-provoking allegory is a powerful encouragement never to forget that God's Word brings joy and hope to His children even in affliction. *Be joyful in hope, patient in affliction, and faithful in prayer.* (Romans 12:12)

Martha Bent
Co-Founder, Essential Piece Ministries International

Barbara Coleman has written an accessible and compelling account of her battle with chronic pain. It is an instructive story of growing self-knowledge and deepening faith. Both those dealing with chronic pain and those living with people who suffer from chronic illness will find valuable insight in this book.

Susan C. Bourque
E.B. Wiley Professor of Government,
Emerita Provost and Dean of the Faculty,
Emerita Smith College, Northampton, MA

This little book (in allegorical form) contains short chapters of insight that the author has gleaned from living with suffering. Take time to ponder the contents. Whether we describe our lives as easy or difficult, every reader will find Barbara Coleman's *The Wonderful Land of Affliction* instructive. The subject matter is both simple and profound, truthful and thought-provoking. May our minds dwell on such things, and may the result be that we grow in wisdom, gentleness, and forbearance!

Tricia Bloomberg
Women's Ministry Coordinator, Reformed Presbyterian Church of Bowie
Bowie, Maryland

Barbara writes a compelling piece interweaving the struggles of those with chronic illness. She writes with empathy and understanding of the grief, anger, hurt, contentedness, and joy that are all part of the journey. The common thread on her journey is the steadfast love of Jesus, her Savior, and His hand holding hers as He guides her safely through. I am a grandmother now and have lived in this Land of Affliction since I was 17. I wish I had had this story to guide me and share with others when they tried to understand!

Peggy Parker
Friend and fellow sufferer, Annapolis, Maryland

God has specially equipped Barbara to write about the beauty and treasures found in the Land of Affliction. She knows of the wonders God performs in people there to make it a lovely place to spend time. She has spent many years in that land with Jesus, being made beautiful in spirit and truth. Read and be touched by God, who makes beautiful what is not, who cares for the afflicted, and who creates such beauty in them! Go, care for the afflicted as Jesus did, learn beautiful and wonderful things from them, and be blessed by their stories.

Peggy Locher
Friend and fellow pilgrim

Bono (the lead singer of U2) says the best way to make an album is to "open up a vein." Barbara Coleman opens up a vein in *The Wonderful Land of Affliction*. She pours out her pain journey as a path toward the type of spiritual knowledge often gained by suffering. Using the time-tested method of allegory, the author allows us to walk in the shoes of the afflicted. The journey is not lonely; she – and we – meet with different characters, each holding a unique perspective for interpreting lifelong pain. Coleman's allegory reveals what it is to suffer without oversharing. I commend it to all who minister, for we rarely know if or what type of pain the people around us are enduring.

Rev. Nicholas Hathaway
Associate Pastor, New Covenant OPC

The Wonderful Land of Affliction

EXPLORING ADVERSITY THROUGH ALLEGORY

©2024 by Chronic Joy
Chronic Joy Publishing, Waukesha, WI 53188
chronic-joy.org

Copyright ©2024 by Chronic Joy Publishing
Copyright fuels accessibility, making room at the table for all.
We are grateful you have purchased an authorized edition of
this book, thereby supporting the mission and ministry of
Chronic Joy. We are also grateful for your compliance with
copyright laws by not reproducing, scanning, or distributing
any part of this book in any form without permission.

First Edition: July 2024
Printed in the United States of America
ISBN: 979-8-9911077-0-9

All Scripture quotations, unless otherwise indicated, are taken
from the ESV® Bible (The Holy Bible, English Standard Version®),
copyright © 2001 by Crossway, a publishing ministry of Good
News Publishers. Used by permission. All rights reserved.

Other Scripture references are from the following sources:
The Holy Bible, New Living Translation, Copyright © 1996, 2004, 2015
by Tyndale House Foundation. Used by permission of
Tyndale House Publishers, Inc. All rights reserved.
The Common English Bible, © Copyright 2011 Common English Bible.
Used by permission. All rights reserved.

Cover and interior design by Pamela Piquette
Cover image (Stairway to Heaven) by Barbara Coleman
Edited by Jan VanKooten

CHRONIC JOY ABIDE

Chronic Joy®
Ministering to those affected by chronic illness,
mental illness, chronic pain, and disability.

The Wonderful Land of Affliction

EXPLORING ADVERSITY THROUGH ALLEGORY

Chronic Joy®
Waukesha, Wisconsin

Dedication

To Joni Eareckson Tada, whose life, work, and words long ago forged my deep desire to trust God more, and to the one holding this book: I pray that as you read, it will enlighten and encourage your heart, mind, and soul.

Contents

FOREWORD: Joni Eareckson Tada   1
INTRODUCTION: 5

CHAPTER ONE: Moving Day   7
CHAPTER TWO: Miss Joy   11
CHAPTER THREE: Miss Wisdom   17
CHAPTER FOUR: Madam Mercy   21
CHAPTER FIVE: Mr. Patience   25
CHAPTER SIX: Quiet Days   29
CHAPTER SEVEN: Lady Peace   33
CHAPTER EIGHT: Young Courage   39
CHAPTER NINE: Mrs. Unaware   45
CHAPTER TEN: Final Days   49
POSTSCRIPT   51

Reflection Questions   55
References   59
Acknowledgments   63

The Ministry of Chronic Joy   65
Printables   67
Chronic Joy Store   68
Thrive Study Series   69
Abide Study Series   70
Companion Resources   71
Explore Series   72
Books We Love   73

Barbara Coleman

Look from circumstances to the hand that guides and
overrules them; it is your Father's hand, and His
hand is moved by His heart, which heart glows
with unutterable love to you. He is at work
for you, and "none can stay his hand."
(Rev. James Smith)

Foreword

By Joni Eareckson Tada
Joni and Friends International Disability Center

Before You Begin...

The other day, Barbara Coleman and I bumped into each other on the corner of Misery Boulevard and Mercy Lane. We are long-time residents of the Land of Affliction and occasionally cross paths at Misery and Mercy.

Visitors to our Land will often stop and ask us for directions. Misery Boulevard is a dead-end street, so we urge them to turn up Mercy Lane, where eventually they will find restful inns and green pastures beside still waters – but few choose that way. Newcomers usually take Misery, given that the boulevard is bustling with people who seem to know where they are going. So, Barbara and I do not tarry on the corner. No matter how miserable our pain, we smile, link arms, and take the little Lane to Mercy

Okay, enough of my imaginings.

It's just that Barbara's clever allegory is so winsome and engaging that we feel compelled to explore her hard but happy Land of Affliction – and if we go exploring, we cannot have a better guide than my friend, Barbara Coleman. For decades, she has lived with the mental, emotional, and physical ravages of intractable pain, so she understands misery all too well. However, mercy defines her gentle heart, stalwart character, and deep, abiding friendship with Jesus Christ.

Barbara and I have known each other since childhood, having grown up in the same church and with many of the same friends (I attended kindergarten with her husband, Mike). After I broke my neck and became a quadriplegic, and after I developed cancer and chronic pain, we grew even closer. Our common experience with affliction knitted our hearts together as nothing else.

Nowadays, in our culture of entitlement, there are Christians who diminish the role that suffering plays in shaping a believer's life. They try to explain it away, escape it, avoid it, divorce, medicate, or surgically get rid of it... anything but learn how to live by grace with it. However, Barbara's little book was written for realistic people who want to do more than survive in suffering; they reach for the possibility that they might thrive in affliction.

So, if, in your hardships, you find yourself vacillating between misery and mercy, relax into the following pages. In this sweet allegory (reminiscent of *The Pilgrim's Progress*), you will meet friends who empathize with you. You will glean wisdom that will help temper your pain. What's more, in *The Wonderful Land of Affliction*, you will not be alone – you will have Barbara Coleman and me as neighbors.

Incidentally, I once asked Barbara where she imagined living in the Land of Affliction. "I live in a small cottage on a lane that leads to a tree-filled park," she said. "I sit on a bench there in the morning. This is where I meet with you, Joni. From my yard, I see the bright light of Heaven sometimes peeking between the clouds. Jesus often holds my small hand as He walks and talks with me down the lane."

Those words that paint a consummate picture of peace were uttered through jaw-breaking pain. Amazing! So, Friend, do not plow through this small but significant book too quickly. Read its lessons prayerfully and act on its counsel intentionally. *The Wonderful Land of Affliction* will not lessen your pain, but it can help you make peace with it.

One more thing—remember that Barbara said she lived on a lane in the Land of Affliction? I bet her cottage is just past the green pastures of Mercy Lane.

Barbara Coleman

Mercy will always balance Misery.
(Charles Spurgeon)

Introduction

The one thing I knew all my life was that I would never write a book. I was blessed with the gift of gab but not writing. Extraordinary people write books, and I was more defined by humor, heart, and a little bit of art. Creating has always been my passion, and although I have received awards for gardening and floral design, painting on canvas is my happy place now. My early life was lovely: a comfortable childhood, a blissfully happy marriage, three great sons, and sharing Christ with others through ministry. Easy-peasy. That all changed suddenly when, at 35 years old, I became strangely ill. Over time, I bewildered dozens of doctors in many states and spent a mountain of moolah only to be medically misdiagnosed; hence, the diseases were left untreated for 30 years. During that time (by God's grace and mercy), my soul grew deeply in love with my precious Savior, Jesus Christ. As decades passed, my health continued to decline until finally (30 years almost to the day of onset), the proper tests revealed all. It wasn't pretty. When a body breaks down for decades, it becomes quite fragile and sometimes refuses the rigorous treatments necessary for healing. Now, as a grandma, I am finally under good medical care, but the daily, painful journey continues as I have accumulated 20 diagnoses along the way. So, I ask you, dear reader, why would a suffering, broken-down grandma write a book? The answer is simple: the Lord led me to do it. When I was young and living a life of ease, I never knew how to react to suffering people. To my shame, I didn't learn how to speak to them or care for them. I didn't know how to listen to them, try to understand, or show genuine sympathy.

Then, it was my turn to suffer. My journey was more like the ocean tide coming ashore and slowly eating away at the marvelous, large sandcastle a child had created with his dad, each incoming wave washing a little bit more of the creation out to sea until there was just a lump of wet sand left. Almost every day for three decades, I felt I lost some ground; I was slowly going down. I was a lump of wet sand. How do you explain that to folks who can't comprehend what you're saying? Their eyes glaze over.

My life before and after illness was such a contrast, and I wanted some way to reconcile it. How could I tell the story of the two divergent worlds I had lived in? How could I inspire and equip those living in the Land of Ease and those living in the Land of Affliction to better recognize, accept, understand, love, and serve each other? My friend, Pamela Piquette (co-founder of Chronic Joy Ministry and master encourager), knowing my heart's desire, said, "Barbara, just write it, and we will publish it." The writing began. Dear reader, I wish I could express how my faithful Father in heaven used His mighty power in His broken but willing child to write what you hold in your hand! Although my strength of memory and recall was declining, the Lord's grace was portioned out to me. Despite chronic pain, cognitive fatigue, and confusion, He gave me the thoughts and the words to write this little book, countless short sessions at a time. Truly, I have an extraordinary God!

Chronic Joy, a ministry I love,
will receive all the royalties from this little book.

CHAPTER ONE
Moving Day

I well remember the day I packed my bags to move to the Land of Affliction. I had lived in the Land of Ease for 35 years, and, to tell you the truth, I took most things for granted. I never fully appreciated that I could just pick up and leave the house and go wherever my little heart desired. My life up to that point had been effortless, simple, and with few difficulties. Then, the pain arrived like an unwelcome guest that settles in and decides never to leave. It became increasingly difficult to function like I used to in the Land of Ease, so it was appointed that I should head to the Land of Affliction.

As I approached the gate, I saw a quote engraved in the stone above the entry. It read, "Those who suffer are deemed worthy by the King." I must confess that I was scared at the beginning of this journey. This was a whole new world for me, but I did have some measure of hope when I saw the sign. I was deemed worthy by the King. The King? I was so glad to be reminded that the King lives here in the Land of Affliction and that I am His daughter.

I did not sleep well the first night. Really, who am I kidding? No one ever sleeps well here. In the Land of Ease, sleep came so easily. I would lie down at night, and very soon, it would be morning. Effortless. However, in this new land, sleep was difficult for everyone. All through the night, you might see lights turned on at various times in various rooms, folks trying to cope with their infirmities the best they could. It does not take long to realize that even though *you* want to sleep, afflictions seldom do.

The next morning, I walked around the small town. I saw many people with obvious physical impairments. The thought struck me, "Perhaps I don't belong here. Perhaps the King made a mistake. Maybe I am just a temporary guest." But then I saw people who looked perfectly fine. They seemed quite ordinary – like me. I realized we were the folks with Invisible Illnesses. (Some afflictions cannot be seen with the eyes, such as chronic pain, emotional distress, and mental brokenness.) However, as I got to know people better, I realized it didn't matter whether an ailment was visible or not. We all shared the same thing: a sense of loneliness and grief. All of us were grieving for our old lives.

We were far from what we had known and from our typical daily routines. We had experienced enormous losses. Many of us had lost our jobs, lost our energy, lost touch with friends, lost the ability to care for ourselves, lost our independence, lost riches, pleasures, dreams, and children, and even lost the capacity to think clearly.

It was overwhelming and confusing at first. Growing up, I always thought afflictions were for older people, but looking around, I saw people of all ages and backgrounds. You can imagine my surprise when I saw many children, even very small ones, with various ailments. I found it interesting that their parents were always with them. I finally realized, "Of course, as a parent, you bear your child's affliction as heavily as if it were your own." They lived here with their children, here in the Land of Affliction.

As the days passed, I was welcomed warmly by the permanent residents. Each of them immediately showed deep care and understanding. It was reassuring to learn I didn't have to explain myself. They understood. They understood I was suffering, and they comforted me. My favorite times were when they would share Words of Wisdom from the King.

Nothing better.

Barbara Coleman

Remember this: had any other condition been better for you than the one in which you are, divine love would have put you there.
(Charles Spurgeon)

CHAPTER TWO
Miss Joy

I began visiting the small park near my new home during my first week there. One day, I was sitting on a well-worn bench with a serene lake view when a lovely lady rolled up in a motorized wheelchair. She turned her chair to look at me and smiled, saying, "Hi, my name is Joy. Mind if I park here?"

I answered, "I don't mind at all; in fact, I would love the company."

Joy looked at me briefly and said, "Are you new here?"

"Yes," I replied, "How did you know?"

"Well, I know most of the folks around here because I've been here quite a while, and I get around," Joy said, lovingly patting her wheelchair.

"How long is quite a while?" I asked.

"Over 35 years," she said.

"Wow!" I replied, "That's a long time to be in a wheelchair."

Joy agreed, and then she began to tell me of the accident she had when very young. "When I first came home, I was depressed and in shock," Joy admitted, "I thought my life was over, and I was only a young girl. My family didn't know what to do with me; I was so cranky and uncooperative. Adjusting to the wheelchair was horrible. Folks became uncomfortable around me and treated me differently in the chair. Some people suppose if you can't walk, you can't think. I was still me, with the same personality, after all, but now, I needed help from others and had lost control of my life. I was miserable and frustrated."

"One day, an older lady from a block away visited me." Joy continued, "My Mom brought her into my bedroom and introduced her as Friend Faithful. At first, she simply sat with me. I tried to ignore her for a while, but she kept smiling. Slowly, we began to talk. She was lighthearted and fun. At the end of her visit, I asked her if she would return. Faithful said, 'Yes, my sweet Joy, I will visit you.' Little did I know that meeting her that day was to change my life forever."

"Really?" I exclaimed, "How so?"

Joy explained that Friend Faithful visited her several times a week for months and read the Bible to her. Joy said, "Faithful would explain all the stories to me and tell me of her deep love for her *Great and Awesome God*. Eventually, she introduced me to the Lord Jesus."

"Faithful taught me to pray, so I prayed every night that God would heal me and release me from this chair. Over time, I realized that He decided not to heal me yet; instead, He would use me in my weakness to bring Him glory. [1] *The Lord of All the Earth* promised to slip His hand in mine and walk close to me every day – and He has." [2]

While Joy talked about how she came to live in this land, she smiled radiantly. She was happy.

I always looked forward to my talks in the park with Joy and her ever-present smile. I realized I had met a woman after God's own heart. When I left her, I always felt uplifted in spirit and a bit more content with my own situation. I tried to adopt her adage, "It is better to have a healthy soul in a broken body than to have a broken soul in a healthy body."

Truth!

On one of these days in the park, I confessed to Joy that I sometimes wondered If I could ever do something to lose God's love. Joy patiently said, "God doesn't love you because of what you've ever done or will do. In fact, He set His love on you before you ever did anything. He made this decision even before the beginning of time. [3] God loves you because of what His Son has done. Jesus died in our place so that we can live forever – we lay all our sins on Him, and He will cover us with His perfect righteousness." Joy leaned closer and said softly, "This is how we can know God loves us." [4]

I sat quietly for a while, absorbing what she had said. Joy went on, "See, Sweetie, there is nothing you can do to earn God's favor. God says it's His gift – the gift of salvation. There is absolutely nothing you can bring to Him." Joy paused, "Well, except your need." [5]

"But Joy, since you have this gift of God's love and you love Him back, do you ever wonder why He won't heal you now?"

"Well," she answered, "that would be quite a long discussion about God's sovereign and perfect will." Just then, Joy looked around and said, "I think we'll need to move under the tree because I'm getting so hot here in the sun." She moved her joystick, but nothing happened. Joy said, "Oh, no! I'm going to need some help."

"Sure," I said. "What should I do?"

"See if something is wrong around the motor," replied Joy.

I checked under the rear of her wheelchair and saw a cord hanging down. I plugged it in and declared, "You're good to go!"

After we settled under the tree, Joy said, "We were discussing God's will and trusting that it is always infinitely better than our own. This is a perfect illustration. I could not have fixed my chair today and would have been sitting in that hot sun for hours. However, in His wisdom and kindness, the Lord provided you.

I know it sounds strange, but the only peace I have ever found is desiring God's will above my own. Truly, having Christ's presence and promises is more precious to me than walking again." Joy continued, "You see, my new friend, if God is glorified, all is well. If He is exalted and made known in my life, my well-being need not concern me too much." (6)

Joy was one of the most powerful believers I had ever met. I felt certain that she would lead many souls to Heaven with her compelling witness. (7)

This is the most dangerous trial of all when there is no
trial, and everything goes well; for then a man is
tempted to forget God, to become too bold,
and to misuse times of prosperity.
(Martin Luther)

Barbara Coleman

Every trial is necessary for our good, is ordained by eternal love, and is continued just as long as requisite, but not one moment longer. Every saint needs trials, and every saint is tried. If the Lord intends to make us holy, He will put us into the fire.
(Rev. James Smith)

CHAPTER THREE
Miss Wisdom

Walking home from the park one day, I heard singing from a tiny house window. I stopped by the gate and called out, "Hello!" The singing stopped, and I heard a soft voice say, "Won't you come in?"

I thought to myself, "Why not?" I opened the gate and went up to the door. Opening it slowly, I heard, "It's okay, just come into the bedroom." Entering the tiny, orderly room, I saw an older woman lying on a single bed. She had a colorful quilt covering her that looked handmade and a tattered Bible right beside her.

"Hi," I said. "Your singing is lovely."

"Thank you, you are so kind," she said. "My name is Wisdom. I have seen you pass by from time to time. Do you go to the park?"

"Yes, I love it there, don't you?" I asked.

"Well, I'm sure I *would* love it, but I haven't been out of this room for 40 years." Hearing this shocked me, but I hoped I didn't show it.

"Are you lonely?" I asked.

"Oh no, dear, I have the Lord of All the Earth! I have His friendship and fellowship, His caring and closeness. Every day, I enjoy my Maker's total forgiveness and unconditional, eternal love! Really, what more could I ever want? What you see here," she patted her bed, "is the Lord's perfect plan for my life. He has taught me to be content." [8] I had never heard anyone in Miss Wisdom's fragile, confined condition say they were content.

"How have you done this?" I asked.

"Done what, dear?"

"Well, learned it, you know, learned to be content with your world so small in this tiny room?"

Wisdom smiled, and her face lit up. "Well, it's because of the Good Shepherd," she said. "He is the one who loves me most and is all-wise in everything He does. You see, dear, it is the Lord our Shepherd who chooses the pasture for us, not the sheep! (9) Thank goodness for that because in the past, I did not make the best choices."

"What do you mean?" I asked.

Wisdom looked serious, then quietly said, "I was a fool. I lived for myself, took no interest in others, held no regard for my neighbors, and had absolutely no time for religion. I was self-absorbed. They say whatever you think most about in a day, that is your god, and there was nothing more important in my life than me."

I looked surprised, then asked, "What changed you?"

"Not what, but who," Wisdom replied. "In His abundant mercy, my Heavenly Father saved me from my wretchedness. I was halfway through my life and had failed at everything. I was ashamed and didn't know where to turn or who I could trust. I had no idea what to do for the rest of my life. That is when I was saved. The all-wise God took away my sin and gave me His righteousness. It's called 'The Greatest Exchange.'"

Miss Wisdom's candor profoundly moved me, and I spent the rest of the afternoon with her. While I was there, other folks stopped by. She had a kind, encouraging, and wise word for each one. At one point, she reached for her well-worn Bible, and a part of it fell on the floor.

Someone close by handed her the dropped pages. Wisdom just giggled and remarked, "As the saints said, 'A Bible that is falling apart usually belongs to someone who isn't.'" We all laughed together.

For the next few hours, I just sat there, amazed that such a little person in such a small, sparse room could have such a big effect on so many. I made it my habit to stop in to see Miss Wisdom often because she was so helpful in helping me understand the total acceptance of every hard thing that comes our way. I realized how much I needed Wisdom in my life.

We all do.

Barbara Coleman

Affliction enlivens the spirit of prayer;
Jonah was asleep in the ship but
at prayer in the whale's belly!
(Thomas Watson, paraphrased)

CHAPTER FOUR
Madam Mercy

A few weeks later, I went to the local store. While there, I saw a lovely middle-aged woman also shopping. We passed each other in the produce section, and as I was leaving, I saw her drop her bag of peaches; they scattered everywhere. She stood still, holding onto her cart, looking at all the scattered fruit as her eyes filled with tears. I quickly went over to help her gather the peaches. As I bent over to put them all back into the bag, she said, "Oh, thank you very much!" I looked up and wondered why she wasn't helping. I handed her the bag and said, "You're welcome." "I'm so clumsy," she said, "I seem to be dropping many things lately." "Well, I'm glad to help," I responded.

"My name is Mercy," she said, wiping her eyes. "I am glad to meet you and so grateful you were willing to help me. My husband wondered if I could do the shopping alone, and I told him, 'I'm fine, dear, no problem at all.' But I think it is time for me to admit there *is* a problem." I noticed she was still holding tightly to the cart.

"Look," I said, "Why don't you let me walk you home?"

"That would be so helpful and very kind," sighed Mercy. "I only live around the block."

She was right; it was a short walk. I carried her bags, and she rested her hand on my arm for balance. When we arrived at Mercy's home, she invited me for a cup of tea, which I gladly accepted. I helped her put her groceries away, and we talked about our lives over tea. It turned out Mercy had a progressively debilitating condition caused by a doctor's error decades earlier.

She explained, "There seems to be a little less of me every day."

"I'm so sorry to hear that – really, I am!" I replied. "Are you angry? Are you bitter toward that doctor?"

"Well, I was for years, but my bitterness brought me only sadness and more grief," began Mercy. "The doctor did injure me, and I am suffering because of that. Do you know that he never said he was sorry?" Mercy looked down at her hands in her lap.

Finally, she said, "Since I have received complete forgiveness and immeasurable mercy from my Maker, how can I not extend that to others? So, I have. My trust is in my Creator, the Father of Compassion. I always try to think well of God and every condition He is pleased to bring to me. He has promised that suffering will produce hope in me – and so it has." (10)

Just then, an older man came slowly into the room. He smiled at me, but it looked like a broken smile, kind of sad. He kissed Mercy on the cheek.

Mercy announced, "This is my husband, Pastor Truth."

Pastor Truth sat down, and we told him about Mercy's trouble at the store and why I was there.

Turning to me, Pastor Truth said, "Thank you for blessing my precious wife today. We are both in a season of struggle and sorrow, and you met a very real need this morning. I believe when we have any need, the Lord, the creator and re-creator, gains an opportunity to display His power, wisdom, and love to us. He has done so today through you. Thank you. I … I hope to see you again sometime."

With that, Pastor Truth got up and slowly left the room. I looked at Mercy.

She shrugged and said, "That's the most he has said in days. He struggles with anxiety and depression. It has been this way for a while, so we had to come home from the mission field. Normal daily activities became a source of fear. Most days, he couldn't leave his office. He stopped talking. Everything just became too much – but one thing I know: he loves the Lord, and the Lord loves him."

I held Mercy's hand for a while, not speaking.

I was beginning to see that affliction knew no bounds. Here in the Land of Affliction, there were rich and poor, old and young, from all walks of life, from all countries – including pastors, ministers, Bible teachers, and missionaries. I realized that living with unrelenting adversity is a great equalizer. We all stand on level ground at the foot of the cross.

Barbara Coleman

Every trouble is intended to endear
Jesus to your heart.
(Rev. James Smith)

CHAPTER FIVE
Mr. Patience

The days were turning warmer, and I was finally getting to know my neighbors. A house two doors down had a lovely garden in the front yard. Early one morning, I saw an older man bent over and working in his garden, so I stopped to meet him. He heard my greeting, set down his clippers, and straightened to greet me – but he only straightened halfway. As he walked toward me, a bit bent over, I was struck by his quick smile and shining eyes.

He said, "Hi, I'm Mr. Patience."

"Hi," I said. "I love your garden; it's the nicest I've seen in a long time."

He thanked me and asked if I would like to sit on his garden bench for a while. After we sat down, Mr. Patience took off his gloves and laid them down. That is when I saw his hands. They were sad hands, so swollen and deformed. He saw me staring and kindly said, "Oh, don't mind these old hands. I have a deforming disease, and my body doesn't look like it used to."

"That must be so very painful," I said. "How are you able to work in the garden?"

"I can only work for a few minutes at a time, and then I sit and rest," he replied. "Then I start up again. I love it so much; I love working in the soil and caring for my plants. It makes me feel closer to the Creator."

"Oh yes, I understand that – but don't you have any help? Do you have someone who will care for your garden in the future? Or..." I hesitated, "care for *you* in the future?"

"Well, I used to be married," said Mr. Patience. "Not happily, but that was my fault. I wasn't a nice man. I was intolerant, always complaining. My wife, though, was a sweetheart. She was always patient and kind to me. Best of all, she would pray for me. Then, only six months before she died, Jesus, my dear, adorable Savior, came into my life." He smiled at me, and I could see his eyes had filled with tears.

"So, I'm by myself now," Patience went on, "but I don't ever think of myself as being alone. I always have the Lord with me. If I need strength here in my garden, I ask Jesus if I can borrow some. He has strength to spare. After all, He is my Rock of Refuge, my Strong Fortress. Oh yes, I don't need to fret about anything. [11] After all, worrying is a form of unbelief."

Mr. Patience and I talked for a long time. He was eager to share his life with me. It turned out that he had many crosses to bear since he became a widower—many more than the ones I could see with my eyes. He spoke of the high privilege of carrying a cross because he said it made him more conformed to his Savior.

"Do you know what I wonder?" I asked.

"What?" Mr. Patience said. I started boldly, "How did you accept it when your body began to break down, um, I mean, when you lost your normal abilities and became weak?" I paused. "Oh, dear," I mumbled, "I suppose I'm trying to ask if you ever questioned why God allowed this." I touched his hands gently.

Mr. Patience sat looking at my soft little hand lying on his large, misshapen ones and then responded. "My friend, what I've come to understand is that *what God takes from me is less than I owe Him, and what He leaves me is more than I deserve."*

I liked Mr. Patience from the first moment we met. He was easy to talk to and had such rich stories to tell that I didn't want to go home.

Mr. Patience mentioned he had almost no family left, only one daughter. "She lives in the Land of Ease," he said, "not too far away. I recently called her and asked her to come for a short visit because I hadn't seen her for a very long while (He paused.), really, since last year."

"Did you have a good time?" I asked excitedly.

"Well," Patience responded, "she said she had to sort some clothes to give to charity, so perhaps she would come another time."

When I heard what his daughter said, I was overcome with disbelief and, yes, other exceedingly uncharitable things that I should not have been thinking. How could anyone not want to come to visit this dear man? Sort some clothes?! What a pitiful excuse!

Barbara Coleman

What God takes from me is less than I owe Him,
and what He leaves me is more than I deserve.
(William Gurnall)

CHAPTER SIX
Quiet Days

If you visit the Land of Affliction for a day, you will first notice the pace. Everything moves at an easy, gradual, intentional pace. I do very little … and do it slowly. Most of us use all our energy just to figure out how to make it through the day.

Over time, I became frustratingly aware of my weaknesses. It is humbling when you simply cannot do what you used to do. However, the good news is that any time I accomplished anything (like making dinner, walking to the mailbox, or even taking a shower), I knew I was aided by divine strength… strengthened by the King.

This is acceptable service.

I began to realize that in my younger days, while living in the Land of Ease, I was often stunned when I experienced hardship. I now saw that hardship had been like boot camp, a training time, preparing me for the journey ahead – preparing me for suffering. I began to trust the God of Providence more, assured He never makes mistakes in the intensity or timing of our suffering. I was starting to understand Paul's words when he wrote: "I can do everything through Christ, who gives me strength." (12)

Another thing you might notice if you visited me in the Land of Affliction was that I didn't look anything like I did in the Land of Ease. The changes weren't only physical; I was different on the inside. There just seemed to be less of the old me. It was like I was fading.

When I lived in the Land of Ease, everything seemed so important and urgent, but now God used affliction to draw me near and enabled me to loosen my tight grasp on the world. Gone was the desire to be in everyone else's business. Gone was the energy to accomplish grand feats, especially to please others. It was as if I had been emptied so I could be filled unexpectedly with an abundance of quiet and peace. (13)

This was a good thing.

During these quiet days, I walked with, talked to, and worshiped the Lord. He held me very close. Precious friend, allow me to tell you what it is like to be held close by the Lord.

Living with unrelenting pain or sorrow fills long nights with despair. There are no distractions at night, no one to bear your burden – except, of course, the One who never sleeps. Early in my journey, when pain would wake me, I began the habit of letting my heart and mind go to Jesus and picture myself climbing into His lap. He would place His left arm under my head, and His right arm would embrace me (as He says in His Word (14)). Sometimes, I thought I could smell the scent of His robe.

Delightful.

Jesus would comfort me with His whispered promises and words of love. On thousands of nights, I would fall back to sleep like this in Christ's arms, peacefully content until morning.

Serenity.

This is my advice to you, kind reader: never stray too far from the sound of His voice. (15)

If we could sin more than He could pardon,
then we might have reason to despair.
(Richard Sibbs)

Barbara Coleman

Is Jesus your teacher? Then sit at His feet, treasure up
His words, and show forth His Praise. He says,
"Learn of me." Learn to know Him, love Him,
obey Him, and live upon Him.
(Rev. James Smith)

CHAPTER SEVEN
Lady Peace

On the Lord's Day, I went to church to worship God, my Savior. It was glorious! I don't think I ever heard such magnificent singing in all my life. Of course, a few people could not join in for various reasons. I was one of those – but my heart was singing along, and I was blessed to listen to all the voices praising our Father, the creator and re-creator.

Before I knew the Lord of all the Lands, I used to look at churches like this one and think they were full of perfect, all-the-same people. In time, I understood how wrong I was! The Church, I discovered, is full of an immense variety of folks from various backgrounds and cultures.

Among them were conservatives and liberals, married and divorced, rich and poor, students and grandparents. They all brought an array of struggles with them as they gathered. Their suffering took many forms: debilitating illness, burdened conscience, financial loss, ceaseless anxiety, habitual sin, physical abuse, natural disaster, broken relationships, and even social ostracism or persecution. They were sorely hurting people needing forgiveness and comfort – just like me.

Well, we certainly came to the right place! It is through worship that we are taught how the Son of God so spectacularly loves us. Worshipping the King of Glory became the highlight of my week.

Beyond compare.

After the service, I grabbed coffee and sat at a small table in the Fellowship Hall. I was new, after all, and didn't know many folks.

Then, a tall, older woman came over and asked if she could join me. "Sure," I said. "Please do."

She said her name was Lady Peace. Peace was not shy, and we soon began talking like old friends.

I love it when this happens, don't you?

I asked her how she came to live in this Land. She said, "Well before I came here, I lived in the Land of Ease. I was very active in my Church until I became unwell. Then I started missing a few gatherings and, over time, I could hardly attend at all."

"Oh, dear," I asked, "Certainly they came to visit you, to help you?"

Peace thought for a moment and then said, "You know, I think there were more good intentions than actual visits. However, over the years, the Lord taught me a valuable lesson I don't think I could have learned any other way."

So, Peace began her story.

"This happened a few years after I became ill. I put my dog out very late one night. Standing and waiting for him to return, I saw a beautiful butterfly land on the front porch railing beside me – at night! I had only ever seen butterflies during the day. So, it made me wonder for the first time in my life, 'Where do butterflies go at night?'

Most of us notice things or people when they are right in front of us, but the adage 'Out of sight, out of mind.' is true. In the Church, we are pretty good at noticing folks right in front of us or when something unusual happens – a new baby (Here comes help to watch the kids or clean the house!) or a death (Here come the casseroles!). Sadly, there is a whole group of people who are sometimes missed – people who are always chronically ill, like I was.

People with chronic illnesses can simply be overlooked. They might be folks with invisible diseases, so it can easily slip your mind that they are suffering emotionally, physically, or mentally. When they are first diagnosed, they get the attention of the Church (like the colorful butterfly on a flower). Folks give sincere love, compassion, and comfort then. As time goes by, however, it's like nighttime: you rarely see the butterfly anymore. The chronically ill aren't at Church regularly. They always seem to miss the meetings and events. So, over time, they are forgotten. I was forgotten."

Peace paused to sip her coffee, then went on.

"I have found that chronically ill Christians who have struggled, sometimes for years, often have a very close walk with the Lord. They have become so lonely that they desperately reach out to Him – and He has become their closest friend. Often, their faith can encourage your faith as you see how they trust the Lord amid pain and loss."

I could feel my emotions welling up inside me. It was as if she knew my story but described it better than I ever could.

"The truth is," Peace went on, "folks in the church would be blessed to spend time with the chronically ill. However, in many congregations, we are overlooked or simply laid aside. Many of us are lonely and friend-sick. We have fallen off the radar. No one is asking where the butterfly has gone!"

Just then, an elderly man laid his hand on Peace's shoulder, softly saying, "I'm sorry, Lady Peace, but we are closing up now."

Barbara Coleman

We both looked up and saw the empty room. We were the only ones left. Peace laughed, saying, "Sorry, Elder Kindness. I always seem to be the last one to leave."

Quickly, we collected our belongings and left. As we walked across the parking lot, Peace continued, "Day after day, I would yearn to answer the phone and have someone say, 'I was thinking of you today and wanted to know how you were coping. How can I pray for you?' Sadly, that rarely happened.

The night I saw the butterfly, I stood there for a long time, all these thoughts running through my mind. I didn't blame anyone for forgetting me, but friend, to my shame, I assure you that's exactly how I behaved toward others years ago when my life was full, my energy was high, and my constant thought was not 'How can I just make it through today?'

As a chronically ill person, my world had become very small: I didn't travel far from home, and I did the same things almost every day. This is how we cope. We are in pain and can't always reach out. I am telling you this to share the priceless lesson I learned. We must extend grace to those who don't understand what we are going through. I found the best way to do that is to reach out and encourage another person exactly when you feel YOU need encouragement."

"Do you stay in touch with the people of your old church?" I asked.

"Oh, yes, especially since my husband passed away," Peace replied as she got into her car, "To this day, I love them all dearly, very dearly. After all, I was the pastor's wife."

I stared at Peace, stunned and unable to speak. Then she beeped, waved, and drove away smiling. I stood there dismayed.

It was hard to grasp that a pastor's wife felt her church forgot her.

Later, as I was walking home, I couldn't stop thinking about what Peace had taught me. Extend grace when we may not be receiving it. Extend grace to those in the Land of Ease and the Land of Affliction.

Extend grace to all! (16)

Christianity is not the removal of suffering,
but the addition of grace to endure
suffering triumphantly.
(Thomas Watson)

CHAPTER EIGHT
Young Courage

I was in the habit of visiting Miss Wisdom several times a week. This day, as I approached her door, I saw Sweet Charity walking by, her arms filled with goodies. We waved to each other. Charity was from the Land of Ease, and her kind-hearted mother first brought her to visit us when she was a little girl. She seemed to have an innate ability to see another person's need and know how to fill it. Sweet Charity is married now and, much to our delight still comes to visit us every week.

Everyone I know loves Charity.

During this visit with Miss Wisdom, I met a young 17-year-old man. Wisdom introduced him, saying, "This is Young Courage."

Courage turned and greeted me. "What a handsome fellow!" I thought. When Courage stood and leaned over Wisdom, I heard him whisper, "Goodbye now. Remember to pray for all the orphans." Then, kissing her gently on the cheek, he said, "I love you." He turned to me smiling and said, "It was a pleasure to meet you." Then he slipped out.

"Well," I said to Wisdom, "what a nice-looking fellow! Is he just visiting you today?"

Wisdom answered, "Oh, no, he is not a visitor. Courage lives here in the Land." She could see my furrowed brow as I wondered why a young, healthy fellow was living here in the Land of Affliction.

Wisdom explained, "You can't tell right off, but Courage lives with a broken heart. When he was about 12 years old, his parents finally allowed him to go away to camp for a few weeks in the summer. On the last day, all the campers were ready to go home. The parents began arriving, and the campers were excited to see them and to have them meet their new friends.

As the afternoon wore on, all the campers were reunited with their folks – except Courage. His family didn't show up. It wasn't until later in the evening that word reached the camp that his mom, dad, brother, and sister were all killed in a terrible car accident on their way to pick him up. Courage had lost his entire family on that day.

Over the past five years, he has been learning how to bear this sadness. He truly desires to have the courage of Christ and to look more like the Savior every day. It is a very high privilege to be conformed to Christ." (17)

Wisdom paused and took a deep breath. It looked like she was in pain. She continued, "Oh, yes, my dear, it's these crosses we carry daily that form us into Christ's image. As the Saints say, 'You cannot sneak quietly into Heaven without a cross.'" (18)

After hearing Young Courage's story, I felt like my heart was pierced. I couldn't imagine losing your whole family in one day. I was brokenhearted for this young man and thought of him often.

Several days later, I saw Young Courage sitting at a small table reading a book in the Coffee Shop. I introduced myself, reminding him we met at Miss Wisdom's home the other day. "Can I join you for a few minutes?" I asked.

'Sure,' he said.

"Listen, Courage," I started. "Wisdom told me about you losing your family." I felt awkward and unsure how to approach this extremely sensitive subject.

Young Courage saw my hesitation and said encouragingly, "It's okay, I never mind talking about my journey."

"Well, I was wondering," I began, "if you could help me understand how you coped with the overwhelming, sudden loss." I could feel my eyes filling with tears, and I worked hard to regain control.

Courage said, "I suppose the simple answer is prayer."

"Prayer," I repeated.

"At first, it was the prayers of others for me," he said. "I was 12 years old, what did I know? I didn't know how to mourn. I was angry, confused, and all alone. I made bad decisions, lost friends, almost lost my life. In the hospital, my parent's friends surrounded my bed and prayed – constantly prayed. The fog in my sorrow-filled brain finally began to lift.

My parents had taught me about God since I was young. For my parents, praying was as natural as breathing. They would pray with me and my siblings every night. Sometimes, I thought it was a waste of time, but they never stopped even though they could tell I wasn't much interested. Then, on that awful day, they were suddenly and completely gone."

Young Courage looked away for a minute, composing himself; I lightly touched his arm. Then he continued, "But, you see, my parents left me a gift."

"They left you a gift? What kind of gift?" I asked.

"The best gift," said Courage. "They taught me how to pray to God."

Courage and I sat in silence for a while. I thought he had finished his story, but then he continued. "I have great memories of my father. I remember playing outside one day when I was a little fellow and getting into a fight with some tough kids. I got pushed down and kicked. I went running home as fast as I could, hurt and weeping until I came to the door of our home. I burst through it and saw my dad standing there. I threw my arms around his legs, sobbing into them, telling him everything that happened, everything that went wrong, and asked him to help, just please help."

Young Courage leaned closer to me, saying, "I learned, over time, to do this with my heavenly Father. The way I understand it, the Lord is my Father, and His Son, Jesus, is the door I run through to approach Him. (19)

This door has two purposes. God's love flows to me through this door, and I run to God through this door. This image of running through the 'door' to speak to God has become more real and precious to me over the five years since I lost my family. Losing my whole family was a nightmare that the Lord turned into a blessing. Now, I spend much of my time in the Throne Room with the Lord of the Lands. I go to pray, to weep, to beg, to thank, to lament, to praise, to lay my burdens down before Him. I use the door a lot!"

Young Courage smiled and said, "You see, to this day, when I'm overwhelmed, the loneliness pierces me like a knife. Thinking I can't handle much more, I start up the now well-worn path that my pain and loss have carved out. I run through the door that

Christ's pain and suffering built for me and tell Him everything. I am addicted to prayer and strengthened by it. I don't need to be weak when I have divine strength to flee to, do I?" [20]

"You are right, dear Courage; the Lord is a heart strengthener," I answered. "Thank you, my young friend, for sharing your story with me. I can see that prayer has completely changed your life—first, the prayers of others, then your daily, faithful prayers. May I add, as believers, we also enjoy the prayers of our Savior interceding for us?"

"Amen," said Young Courage. "Prayer allows our souls to get fresh air from Heaven!"

Barbara Coleman

The less we pray, the harder it gets.
(Martin Luther)

CHAPTER NINE
Mrs. Unaware

I received a letter many months after moving to the Land of Affliction. It was from Mrs. Unaware, a former friend I had known in the Land of Ease. She said she was coming to visit me.

"Wow!" I thought. "This is grand and so unexpected." I felt special that this old friend would take the time to see me. I had many things to share with her, especially the news from an early morning phone call I had just received from my doctor, the kind of call no one wants to get. I also wanted to tell her what it was like to live here so near the Lord and how I witnessed the peace of God outweighing the suffering of the brokenhearted and crushed in spirit. (21) I had many things to share with her, and the thought of her visit made me exceedingly happy.

Mrs. Unaware arrived just in time for lunch. She talked continually while we ate. She talked nonstop out on the porch where we had dessert. She talked incessantly and shared stories from her past, reflecting on her husband's successful business, the challenge of raising difficult children, and the constant annoyance of her next-door neighbor, Mr. Lukewarm.

"Oh, I remember Mr. Lukewarm," I finally interrupted. "He used to live here but became increasingly confused and unhappy. One day, he simply packed his suitcase and returned to his old home in the Land of Ease. I saw the gradual change in him when he no longer trusted the Lord. He took no comfort from reading the Word. It seemed the more he delighted in the world and the things of the world, the less he delighted in Christ. (22)

Many of us saw the warning signs. This compelling draw to the wicked side of the world is from the enemy, the evil one who never rests, the fallen angel, the only being I hate – the great deceiver, Satan himself. My friend, I know this to be true: he is the father of lies who sometimes whispers in your ear, 'You can't bear this another day.'" I paused, remembering.

"Mr. Lukewarm," I continued, "eventually desired his former life more than a future life with the promise of Heaven. Sadly, he could not part with the sinful world, so he parted with his Maker." (23)

"I don't know about all that," said Mrs. Unaware impatiently. "I just know he is now a sad, bitter old man, but that's not why I have come to see you today." She smiled and continued, "I was wondering what you are doing for Thanksgiving."

I thought, "Well, isn't this the most lovely, unexpected, considerate act of love? Out of the blue, an old friend had come to invite me to her home for the holiday! How did she know I had nowhere to go? How did she know about my loneliness?"

Grinning from ear to ear, I answered Mrs. Unaware, "Well, I don't have any plans at all. I'm completely available!"

"That's great," she said, "because I wanted to invite you to come to my house to cook for my whole family. This is the first year we can all be together, you see. There will be about nine of us, seven adults and two children. I know that won't be a problem for you because when you used to live near me, you entertained all the time. You are such a wonderful cook and, of course, I will pay you if you want. Could you come early that morning to start setting up?"

I could not speak. It took me a few minutes to fully understand what was happening. This old friend had not come today to be a comfort to me. I realized she hadn't asked how I was doing this whole time. She didn't know about the hard news I had received from my doctor, that my disease was much worse, and my time was now short. [24] She didn't come to hug me or weep with me, ease my pain or promote my joy, lament with me or pray with me. At that moment, I felt marginalized, depreciated, and unloved. [25]

Finally, I could speak, "Let me get this straight," I said. "You are not inviting me to join you for dinner; you are inviting me to cook the dinner."

"Yes, dear," Mrs. Unaware spoke hurriedly, "but I have to know soon because I am on quite a tight timeline."

"I'm sorry, but I have to say no. There are quite a few reasons, though."

"That's okay. I don't need a reason; a no is a no. Now, I really must run."

I walked her to her car. She rolled down her window before pulling away and said, "Now, don't you go feeling too bad about disappointing an old friend. I'm sure I'll find someone else to cook the dinner. I wanted to mention that you're looking kind of pale. You should get out in the sun more. Thanks for lunch."

She drove away with a quick wave and a smile. I waved goodbye, trying to smile, but I was glad she couldn't see my tears.

Barbara Coleman

I have reason to praise (God) for my trials,
for most probably, I should have
been ruined without them.
(John Newton)

CHAPTER TEN
Final Days

I always tried to spend time with Miss Wisdom on my good days. Her life was a Christ-like fragrance drawing me to Heaven. (26) She often said that the unchanging love of the Lord was far better than life itself. (27) That is why I shouldn't have been sad when I heard our Father in Heaven had sent His elect angels to comfort and carry her Home to the Celestial City.

Wisdom was always so wonderful to be with; I can understand why the Lord wanted to have His precious child close to Him. Later, I was told that as she was about to cross over to her heavenly home, those around her bed heard her softly say, "Let the Lord do what seems good to Him." (28) Truly, she was a monument to God's mercy!

Wisdom's death reminded me of what she once told me: "The Master Gardener plants each of us in His garden and cares for us until our work for Him is done. Then we are transplanted to our eternal home."

I was struck with overwhelming sadness and grief at first. I would desperately miss our valuable times together when Miss Wisdom would share her knowledge of the Lord and His ways with me. She had loved me like a daughter. I was miserable for days until I decided that instead of continuing my mourning, I would try to praise and thank God for His mercy, goodness, love, and grace in having given me this special friend. Being grateful for what she taught me was slowly turning my sorrow into joy. As I would pass her empty house on my daily walk to the park, I would rehearse her wise words in my mind:

- ~ The greatest source of joy imaginable is to have your name written in the Book of Life.
- ~ The admission into God's presence is Christ. (29)
- ~ You will need all of eternity to thank God for the day of your salvation.
- ~ Always have someone in your life that loves God more than they love you.
- ~ In affliction, God weans you from loving the world and causes you to yearn for Heaven.
- ~ God will not thank you for doing what He did not ask you to do. (30)
- ~ Contentment is wanting what you already have.
- ~ Afflictions conform us to Christ and prepare us to meet Him.
- ~ Strive to desire God's will above your own.
- ~ Only glance at your problems, but gaze on Jesus.
- ~ Learn to hate what God hates and love what God loves.
- ~ The Lord can only do good all the time.
- ~ When it's hard to pray, simply say: Lord, I love You, I trust You, I thank You.

Quite soon, I was at peace with Wisdom's death. After all, she had been made into the likeness of the King in His Kingdom of light and life and was enjoying unending happiness forever and ever.

That is my hope, too.

Postscript

I have just reviewed what I have written to you, gentle reader, and I can see that you might harbor some fear about coming here to live someday. Put aside those fears. That was never my intention. In fact, it is the opposite.

If you are called, you must come. I admit that adapting to this new home is a process. Along the way, you may wade through resentment and bitterness. You may become exhausted from working so hard just to get through each day. You may tire of your trial when it seems like you're pushing a boulder up the mountain every day. You may become weary of being you – but I promise you all that will be easier if you live in the shadow of the King.

Who doesn't desire a faithful friend who is right there for you when you are desperate, when you have a bewildering problem, or when you encounter overwhelming discouragement? Who doesn't need an advocate with unlimited wisdom, compassion, love, and guidance? Who wouldn't hold close a Savior who will forgive every sin?

That is Jesus.

If you need anything today, go to Jesus. He is ready to help. Unburden yourself. Share your secrets, griefs, and the burdens that (perhaps) no one else knows. My friend, you will be blessed more than I can tell you in this short note.

You may think those of us living here should be pitied. Oh, no, never! We have something very special here that none of us fully enjoyed in the Land of Ease. Every day, we have the luxury of time to walk and talk with the King. Yes, He is remarkably close to us in this Land, even through long, dark nights. Filled with constant needs, we are led to times of sweet fellowship as we develop a constant dependence on the Servant King. He was a Man of Sorrows and acquainted with grief – and He sent us the most amazing gift you could ever want: His precious Holy Spirit.

Oh, I wish I had words to describe to you, my friend, what it is like to have God in the form of the Holy Spirit living in my soul! He provides me with vast stores of peace, joy, and comfort not found anywhere else. This God is a promise keeper; He is present everywhere and condescends to be with us here... never leaving us alone.

What a God!

All of us here know that when you live in the Land of Affliction, you live closer to the King than ever before. That is precisely what makes it so wonderful - *The Wonderful Land of Affliction*!

As time passed, I realized what the King, the mighty God, had known all along. I am never going back to the Land of Ease. This is my home now. He ordained that I should dwell here; I truly believe it was the best thing for me. Living a life of pain changed me like nothing else could. I am now desperate for the Shepherd King, and He draws me close and walks next to me every day – which is a very good thing!

In the early years, because of unrelenting pain, I used to ask the Lord to take me to Heaven every day. Then I realized that was wrong. I needed to trust that His timing was best and that I was to remain here on earth until my work for Him was done.

Yearning for, preparing for, and picturing Heaven is good for the soul. You know, there are some days when I think I can see my heavenly home from here. Jesus has said He is making a special room for me there. How great is that? Recently, it occurred to me that if I lose my battle with this disease and the time comes for my final move, I won't have far to go—I live that close!

The Lord has entrusted me with this story to tell you, dear one. Indeed, there are many other incredible testimonies here in the Land, but I am weary, and my closest friend (named Pain) is demanding my attention. Honestly, I can't remember a day without constant, exquisite pain, so I never thought I could tell my tale. However, the King has laid it on my heart and has helped me write every word you have read.

I am so grateful you have taken the time to read it.

Praying blessings on you wherever you live. By the way, my name is Loved.

Barbara Coleman

The God of Providence has limited the time, manner, intensity, repetition, and effects of all our sickness. Each throb is decreed, each sleepless hour predestined, each relapse ordained, each depression of spirit foreknown, and each sanctifying result eternally purposed. ...The limitation on sickness is wisely adjusted to our strength, to the end designed, and to the grace apportioned. ...the weight of every stroke is accurately measured. ... We cannot suffer too much nor be relieved too late.
(Charles Spurgeon)

Reflection Questions

Chapter One - Moving Day
- Most people do not like change. Do you?
- Have you ever had a drastic change (physical, mental, or emotional) in your life? What helped you cope?
- Do you know someone who is going through that now? Is there some way you could help?

Chapter Two - Miss Joy
- What occurs to you when you see someone in a wheelchair? Does it make you feel uncomfortable or awkward? Do you look away?
- Have you ever wondered how difficult it is for them? Some people suppose, "If you can't walk, you can't think," when, in fact, these folks have learned rich life lessons that could benefit you.
- Would you be comfortable approaching someone in a wheelchair and saying, "Is there any way I could help you?" Consider seizing the opportunity the next time you see someone in a wheelchair.

Chapter Three - Miss Wisdom
- At the end of this chapter, we read that we all need wisdom. What does this mean to you?
- It is one thing to try to gather insight on your own, but being blessed with someone in your life with age and experience is "wise."
- People like Miss Wisdom, who desire to know and love the Lord Jesus more every day, can be some of the best earthly guides you can find. Their suffering has drawn them nearer the Lord, and they are usually sensitive,

discerning, and loving. They can counsel you non-judgmentally, using the Word of God.
- Consider finding a Miss Wisdom and befriend them.

Chapter Four - Madam Mercy
- Madam Mercy speaks of the true forgiveness she has given and received. Do you find it hard to extend forgiveness to others?
- You briefly meet Pastor Truth in this chapter. Have you ever suffered from anxiety or depression? Do you know someone who does?
- Depression is an "invisible" affliction. Unless someone tells you they are suffering, you may not realize it. If someone shares with you that they are dealing with anxiety or depression, what can you do?

Chapter Five – Mr. Patience
- In this chapter, you meet Mr. Patience, a gentle, elderly gardener. He readily confesses, "What God takes from me is less than I owe Him, and what He leaves me is more than I deserve." Is this true for you? In what ways?
- Mr. Patience struggles daily. How could you better understand what life is like for a suffering person? Perhaps ask,
    - "What is it like living with your illness, weakness, disability?
    - What does a typical day entail?
    - Then, really listen!

Chapter Six - Quiet Days
- The narrator describes quiet days as "a boot camp, a training time, preparing me for the journey ahead -

preparing me for suffering." Do you use "good" days like this to prepare yourself for future trials? How?

- What does the narrator mean when she says of God, "Never stray too far from the sound of His voice?"

Chapter Seven - Lady Peace

- Are you living in the Land of Ease? Do you know someone chronically ill? How could you remedy unintentionally forgetting about them and their struggles?
- Are you living in the Land of Affliction and feeling that others have laid you aside? How can you put aside your expectations and extend grace to all?
- What is meant by friend-sick?

Chapter Eight - Young Courage

- Why does Sweet Charity continue to visit those in the Land of Affliction after all these years?
- The story of Young Courage is one of persistent prayer. Do you pray as much as you feel you need? Do you look forward to praying?
- What do you think Martin Luther meant by *"The less we pray, the harder it gets"* in the concluding quote?

Chapter Nine - Mrs. Unaware

- Do you know a believer who has become lukewarm? How could you help them?
- Mrs. Unaware was taking advantage of her friend with no regard for her as a person. Have you ever felt "marginalized, depreciated, and unloved" by someone when you expected the opposite? Remember that Jesus endured this as well.

- What ideas do you have for dealing with self-absorbed people?

Chapter Ten - Final Days
- Which of Miss Wisdom's sayings appeals to you the most? Why?
- Do you have a fear of developing a chronic condition or becoming impaired in some way? What is the first thing you would do?
- Why did the author use many names for God throughout the book?
- Do you better understand the title of the book now?
- Were you surprised by the narrator's name at the end?

References

CHAPTER TWO

1 - *But he said to me, "My grace is sufficient for you, for my power is made perfect in weakness." Therefore, I will boast all the more gladly of my weaknesses, so that the power of Christ may rest upon me.* (2 Corinthians 12:9)

2 - *For I, the Lord your God, hold your right hand; it is I who say to you, "Fear not, I am the one who helps you."* (Isaiah 41:13)

3 - *God shows his love for us in that while we were still sinners, Christ died for us.* (Romans 5:8)

4 - *This is real love—not that we loved God, but that He loved us and sent His Son as a sacrifice to take away our sins.* (I John 4:10, NLT)

5 - *God saved you by his grace when you believed. And you can't take credit for this; it is a gift from God. Salvation is not a reward for the good things we have done, so none of us can boast about it.* (Ephesians 2:8-9, NLT)

6 - *Be exalted, O God, above the heavens! Let your glory be over all the earth!* (Psalm 57:5)

7 - Samuel Rutherford (paraphrased)

CHAPTER THREE

8 - *Not that I am speaking of being in need, for I have learned in whatever situation I am to be content.* (Philippians 4:11)

9 - Thomas Manton (paraphrased)

CHAPTER FOUR

10 - *Not only that, but we rejoice in our sufferings, knowing that suffering produces endurance, and endurance produces character, and character produces hope, and hope does not put us to shame, because God's love has been poured into our hearts through the Holy Spirit who has been given to us.* (Romans 5:3-5)

CHAPTER FIVE

11 - *I love you, Lord; you are my strength. The Lord is my rock, my fortress, and my savior; my God is my rock, in whom I find protection. He is my shield, the power that saves me, and my place of safety.* (Psalm 18:1-2, NLT)

CHAPTER SIX

12 - *I can do all things through him who strengthens me.* (Philippians 4:13)

13 - *Pray this way for kings and all who are in authority so that we can live peaceful and quiet lives marked by godliness and dignity.* (1 Timothy 2:2, NLT)

14 - *Your left arm would be under my head, and your right arm would embrace me.* (Song of Solomon 8:3, NLT)

15 - *My sheep hear my voice, and I know them, and they follow me.* (John 10:27, NLT)

CHAPTER SEVEN

16 - *Let no corrupting talk come out of your mouths, but only such as is good for building up, as fits the occasion, that it may give grace to those who hear.* (Ephesians 4:29)

CHAPTER EIGHT

17 - *We know this because God knew them in advance, and he decided in advance that they would be conformed to the image of his Son.* (Romans 8:29, CEB)

18 - Samuel Rutherford - Public Domain

19 - *I am the door. If anyone enters by me, he will be saved and will go in and out and find pasture.* (John 10:9)

20 - *Have I not commanded you? Be strong and courageous. Do not be frightened, and do not be dismayed, for the Lord your God is with you wherever you go.* (Joshua 1:9-10)

CHAPTER NINE

21 - *The Lord is near to the brokenhearted and saves the crushed in spirit.* (Psalm 34:18)

22 - *Do not love this world nor the things it offers you, for when you love the world, you do not have the love of the Father in you.* (1 John 2:15)

23 - *I know all the things you do, that you are neither hot nor cold. I wish that you were one or the other! But since you are like lukewarm water, neither hot nor cold, I will spit you out of my mouth!* (Revelation 3:15-16, NLT)

24 - *For the righteous will never be moved; he will be remembered forever. He is not afraid of bad news; his heart is firm, trusting in the Lord.* (Psalm 112:6-7)

25 - *He raises the poor from the dust and lifts the needy from the ash heap, to make them sit with princes, with the princes of his people.* (Psalm 113:7-8)

CHAPTER TEN

26 - *For we are the aroma of Christ to God among those who are being saved and among those who are perishing.* (II Corinthians 2:15)

27 - *Because Your steadfast love is better than life, my lips will praise You.* (Psalm 63:3)

28 - *And he said, "It is the Lord. Let him do what seems good to him."* (I Samuel 3:18b)

29 - George Swinnock, Works 1:98-100

30 - William Gurnall, *Complete Armour* 1:279-284

Barbara Coleman

Oh, that I could blot out my name and write
God's name on anything that I accomplish.
(William Gurnall, paraphrased)

Acknowledgments

When I told my sister, Jackie, that I was writing a book, she did not laugh. She read a rough draft and then, handing it back to me, said, "Barbara, this is important. Finish it." Thank you, Sister.

I could not have undertaken this journey without the Puritans. I love their writings and use many of their thoughts and quotes throughout this little book. I can't wait to meet them!

I am deeply indebted to all my Pain Pals who have taught me how to live contentedly in this wearisome but wonderful land of affliction. Perhaps they will see shadows of themselves here.

I'm so thankful for Post-it notes: I couldn't have done this without hundreds of them spread all over our house!

Thank you to all those who gave me feedback and editing suggestions along the way. I would have stopped writing many times except for you (especially Angie!).

I am so grateful to *Chronic Joy Ministry*, especially Pamela Piquette. She invited me to write this little book and guided me along the way. *Chronic Joy* is undertaking the entire publishing challenge and will receive all the profits from this book. To God's glory, this small ministry is making a huge impact in the lives of thousands of suffering folks.

This endeavor would not have been possible without my sweetest sweetheart, Mike, President and sole member of my fan club. He thinks everything I do is the best. You're my favorite! Most especially, I thank my precious Lord, the Living God, the best writer I know. I am weak, but He is strong. I asked Him to please help me – and He did! May this book and its message bring many to love Him more.

Barbara Coleman

God will not thank you for doing that which
he did not ask you to do.
(William Gurnall)

THE MINISTRY OF CHRONIC JOY®

Chronic Joy is *making a difference one precious life at a time.* Perhaps today, that one life is yours!

As a global resource ministry, we are dedicated to compassionately serving all those affected by chronic illness, mental illness, chronic pain, and disability by providing accessible, easy-to-use, faith-based educational resources and publications.

Chronic illness, mental illness, and chronic pain impact every aspect of life: faith, family, finances, friendships, marriage, education, hobbies, and work.

Chronic illness *is* hard, but there *is hope*.

On January 1, 2016, God invited us to take a step of faith to begin a global resource ministry, though we had no idea how to do that nor the scope of what this ministry would become.

In April 2016, we officially became a 501(c)(3) nonprofit (No small accomplishment!), but God was just getting started.

Today, Chronic Joy offers:

- resources for those with chronic and mental illness, caregivers, parents, children, teens, servant-hearted leaders, marriages, and churches.
- more than 100 web pages filled with faith-based, thoughtfully developed, and deeply meaningful content.
- a comprehensive library of curated books.
- 400+ (and counting) audio blogs.
- 250+ free printables – with more great content on the way!

- new posts every week bursting with encouraging, hope-filled, and inspirational stories.
- more than a dozen inspiring prayer pages.
- an extensive collection of free, high-res, faith-based images available for immediate download.
- Chronic Joy Publishing has nine outstanding books (studies, devotionals, and companion resources).

Chronic Joy is a ministry led by God and His word. Luke 6:31 (*Think of the kindness you wish others would show you; do the same for them.* [The Voice]) propels us to continue to develop tools and resources so that those affected by illness and pain can discover radical hope, find Biblical purpose, embrace eternal worth, and encounter God's exquisite joy.

Pamela Piquette
Cindee Snider Re
Co-Founders of Chronic Joy

Chronic Joy is making a difference *one precious life at a time.*

Perhaps today, that ONE life is yours.

The Wonderful Land of Affliction

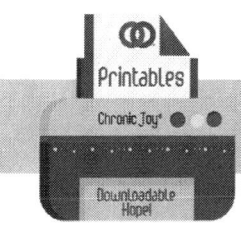

CHRONIC JOY® PRINTABLE PUBLICATIONS

Chronic Joy offers more than 250 beautifully-designed, encouraging, inspirational, FREE printables.

There's **something for everyone**—from *Verses to Comfort and Encourage* to *Promises for Parents*, from *Praying the Psalms* to children's activities, from *33 Biblical One Anothers* to *76 Questions to Connect You as a Couple*.

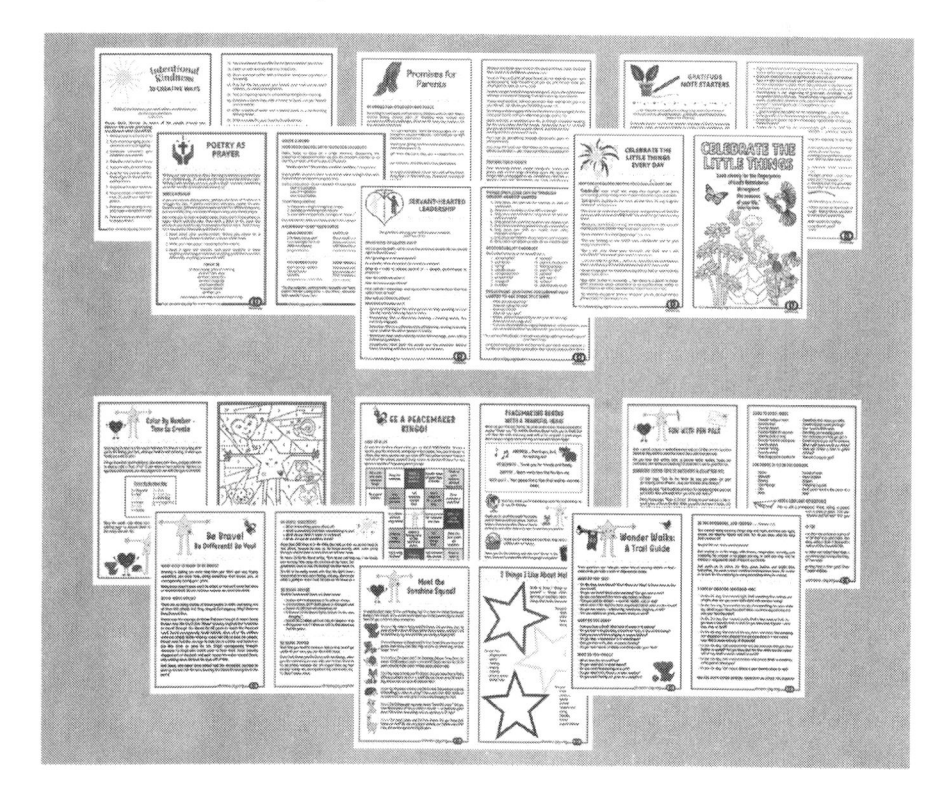

Download a little hope at chronic-joy.org/printables today!

67

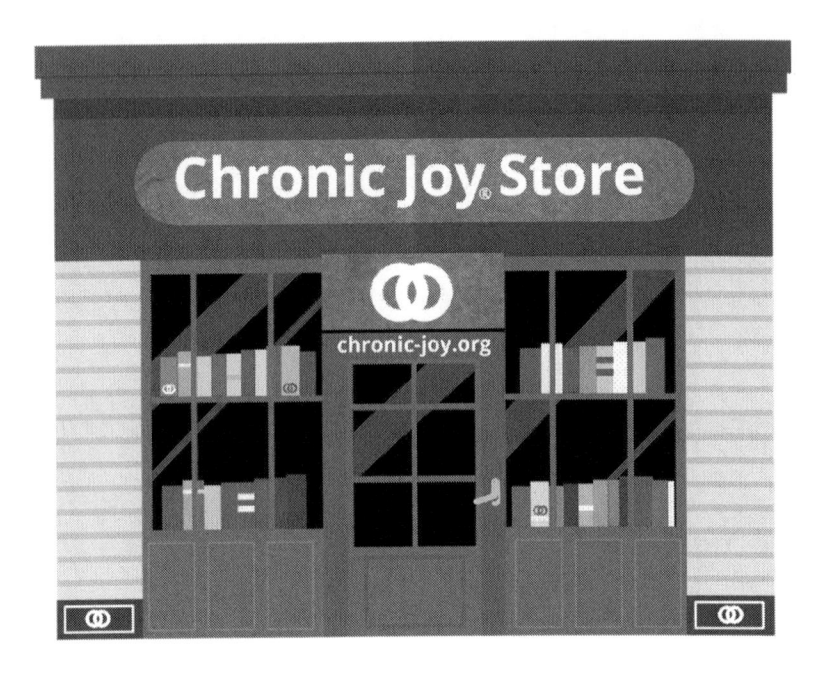

YOUR ONE-STOP SHOP

- Flat Cards
- Professionally Printed Guides
- Service in a Box
- Chronic Joy Book Titles

EVERY PURCHASE MAKES A DIFFERENCE!

shop.chronic-joy.org

CHRONIC JOY — THRIVE SERIES

Each 10-chapter study invites you to discover the imperishable hope rooted in Christ alone, God's precious purpose for your life, and your God-ordained worth.

DISCOVERING HOPE
Beginning the Journey Toward Hope in Chronic Illness
Cindee Snider Re

FINDING PURPOSE
Rediscovering Meaning in a Life with Chronic Illness
Cindee Snider Re

EMBRACING WORTH
Understanding Your Value in a Life with Chronic Illness
Cindee Snider Re

Find our books at shop.chronic-joy.org or on Amazon.

Barbara Coleman

CHRONIC JOY *Abide*

Learn to abide in the love and compassion of Christ.

The Abide Series explores the rich, diverse, and dynamic topics experienced by those affected by chronic illness, mental illness, and chronic pain. Learn what it means to lean into Jesus, to rest on Him, and to pour our hearts out to Him.

Find our books at shop.chronic-joy.org or on Amazon.

CHRONIC JOY® COMPANION RESOURCES

Friends for the Journey

Discover friendly guides for building safe micro-communities, exploring purpose in new ways, discovering creative ideas for service, and growing at the pace of grace.

These topical books streamline concepts into accessible, relatable, **easy-to-use, quick reference resources.**

#PenToPaper
THE ART OF LETTER WRITING
Note Starters For Every Day

SERVANT-HEARTED LEADERSHIP
Called to Listen, Lead, and Love Like Jesus
LISTEN • LEAD • LOVE

Find our books at shop.chronic-joy.org or on Amazon.

CHRONIC JOY EXPLORE SERIES

DEVOTIONAL MEMOIRS

The Explore Series invites you into the presence of Jesus through inspiring vignettes, Scripture verses, reflection questions, prayers, and the real-life stories of those whose lives are affected by chronic illness, mental illness, or chronic pain.

Find our books at shop.chronic-joy.org or on Amazon.

**LOOKING FOR A GREAT BOOK?
LOOK NO FURTHER!**

BOOKS WE LOVE

We've handpicked *outstanding books* just for you!

When you shop through our links,
your purchase helps support
the mission and ministry of Chronic Joy.

**Be inspired and encouraged with outstanding books!
chronic-joy.org/books-we-love**

Made in the USA
Columbia, SC
19 June 2025